BUTTERMERE, CRUMMOCK & WHINLATTER

by
Tom Bowker

DALESMAN

1992

Key to Maps

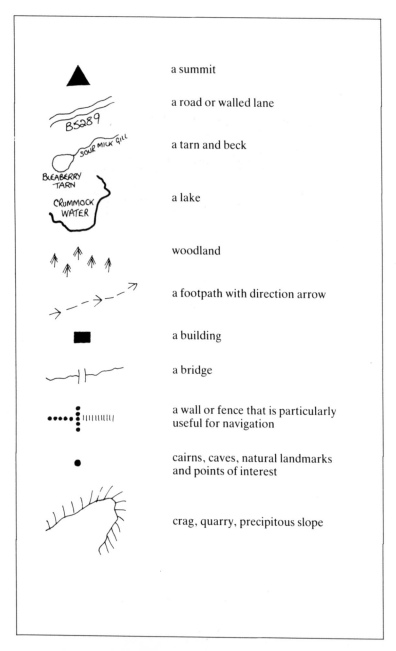

a summit

a road or walled lane

a tarn and beck

a lake

woodland

a footpath with direction arrow

a building

a bridge

a wall or fence that is particularly useful for navigation

cairns, caves, natural landmarks and points of interest

crag, quarry, precipitous slope

Contents

Cover map by Barbara Yates

Sketch maps by Helen Bowker

Dalesman Publishing Company Ltd.,
Clapham, via Lancaster, LA2 8EB

First published 1988
Reprinted 1992

© Tom Bowker, 1988

ISBN: 0 85206 942 1

Typeset by Lands Services, East Molesey, Surrey
Printed and bound by The Lavenham Press Ltd., Lavenham, Suffolk

INTRODUCTION

THIS guide is not for the motorist who is looking for a couple of miles stroll in his driving shoes. Nor is it for the hardened fell-walker. It is written principally for the motorist-cum-walker who is prepared to pull on a pair of boots or stout walking shoes, sling a small pack on his or her back, and be happy to be out for at least two or three hours, or more. Many of the walks described will also appeal to family parties; to those introducing their children to the hills. There are many facets of these walks other than the attaining of summits. There are tarns and pools for bathing, woods, waterfalls, caves and lovely picnic spots, all of which would appeal to children of all ages. Most of the walks are circular, starting and finishing at the same point but returning by a different route in order to add interest. The walks described are roughly divided into three types:–

1. Valley Walks Genuine valley walks are at a premium in Lakeland. This is basically because the nearer to the valley floor the more problem with access over private or farm land, and that the very nature of the terrain eventually forces the walker uphill to some degree. Given dry conditions, all these walks could be done in training shoes but it must be remembered that any Lakeland walk will have its boggy patches, and special care must be taken on the wet or slimy rocks at the edges of streams or waterfalls.

2. Medium Walks These are walks that reach summits that are under two thousand feet in height. They form the bulk of the walks in the booklet for it is felt they would appeal most to the kind of motorist-cum-walker-cum-family party described above. They often, however, cover similar terrain to the fell walks of Section 3 and strictly speaking the same rules about clothing and footgear described in that section apply here. Given dry summer conditions, most of these walks could be done in 'trainers' and in wet conditions 'wellies' would be an asset, but care must be taken on wet or slimy rock or at the edges of streams and waterfalls and stout walking shoes or boots are recommended.

3. Fell Walks These are walks that reach one or more summits over two thousand feet in height. They are not however strenuous walks of their type, either being of no great length or over relatively easy ground, or both. Where there is any possibility of the walker getting into difficulty, easier alternatives are given. Nevertheless these are fell walks and should be treated with respect, especially in bad or winter conditions. I do not wish to labour the point but would not rest easy if I did not enumerate here a few basic rules. It is advisable to wear boots, carry a map, compass, whistle and waterproofs. In winter a torch, gloves, balaclava, spare sweater, a plastic survival bag and spare food are advisable additions. Loose-fitting jeans are okay in summer but warmer covering is advisable in winter. Never be afraid to turn back if the weather deteriorates. If you are forced to use your compass, start using it at a point where you know where you are then you have a fixed point to return to; don't wait until you are lost!

All the walks described are accompanied by a rough sketch-map which used in combination with the text should prove adequate given good weather. It is advisable, however, particularly for the fell walks, also to carry the one-inch O.S. Lake District 'Tourist' Map, or the applicable sheet of the O.S. The English Lakes, 1:25000 Outdoor Leisure Maps. As well as being a better aid to navigation, being more detailed than the sketch map, they also help you to identify the various peaks and lakes seen from a particular viewpoint. All the place names detailed in this guidebook are as given on the 1982 edition North Western area sheet of the above maps. The milages are approximate and 'left' or 'right' refers to an object as if facing it. A note on car parks is included with every walk, but this situation can be somewhat fluid. Local authorities have a habit of restricting parking areas and/or opening up new ones some distance away from those described. So please don't blame the author if a particular parking situation differs from the description; it is as accurate and up-to-date as the author can make it.

All the walks described here are on official rights-of-way, permissive footpaths, or public access areas. Routes can, however, be legally changed from time to time by developments or road improvements, in which case there should be a signpost specifically indicating the alteration.

Before I began this series of booklets my interest had always been with the high fells. As the work progressed, however, I found myself discovering facets of Lakeland that I was unaware existed, despite over thirty years of fell-walking. I became fascinated by hills and footpaths that I must admit I had previously scorned. I only hope that the readers of this booklet discover as much pleasure from these walks as I did. Happy Walking!

Tom Bowker

BUTTERMERE

Walk 1

Fell Walk
7 miles/2600 feet of ascent

The Buttermere Trio

*A delightful ridge walk. Once the crest is gained the going is easy,
with an old fence to aid navigation. The all round views are splendid,
but the 'bird's-eye' view into Bleaberry and Burtness Combes and
upon Buttermere and Crummock Water are superb.*

*Parking: The car park to the right (behind) of the Fish Hotel,
Buttermere (GR 174169).*

TURN RIGHT in front of the Fish Hotel then right again on the path
behind the hotel's private car park. Follow this path across the fields,
ignoring a right fork signposted 'Scale Bridge/Scale Force', towards
the silvery thread of Sour Milk Gill spilling down the wooded flank of
Red Pike. A footbridge takes you over Buttermere Dubs, the beck
linking the lakes. Beyond it a 'Red Pike' sign points left to a smaller
footbridge, followed by a kissing-gate between a wall and fence at the
edge of the lake. Beyond this a path zig-zags up through the trees to a
crossing path signposted Red Pike/Lakeshore.

Now climb the recently rebuilt 'Red Pike' path slanting leftwards
through the trees. It is a solidly constructed piece of work and a vast
improvement on the former eroded trough. Above the tree line the
path climbs left then right up the steep fellside The angle eases as it
passes through an old wall and a threadbare line of equally ancient
trees to reach the bank of Sour Milk Gill. Paths on either side of the
beck lead to the shore of Bleaberry Tarn. Bleaberry Combe is yet
another of Lakeland's elegantly sculpted upland hollows whose
beauty is enhanced by a tarn. It is marred only by the badly eroded
path slashing like an open wound the breast of Red Pike, an
unfortunate fate that all fine fells suffer. Scramble up this steep
mountain highway to reach the cairn capping the summit of Red Pike.
Five lakes, Ennerdale Water, Crummock Water, Loweswater, Buttermere and Derwentwater can be spotted by the vigilant. Arrayed in
splendour across the head of Crummock Water are the lovely

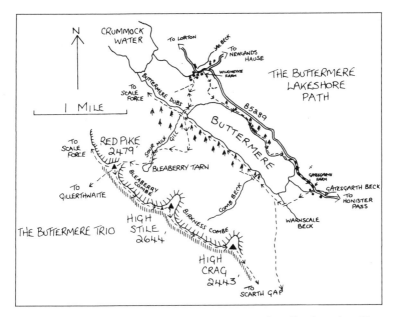

Grasmoor group. Some years ago, on an exceptionally clear day, Ben Lomond was spotted from Red Pike, a distance of 120 miles.

Now head on to High Stile. The rusting remains of an old boundary fence will be met just south of and below the summit of Red Pike. In mist this is a useful aid to navigation as it stays with you all the way until you descend from the ridge. Given good weather keep as close as possible to the precipitous north-eastern rims of these fells for the 'bird's-eye' views of tarn and lakes, often framed between steep gully walls. A pleasant undulating walk of about a mile leads south-easterly around the rim of Bleaberry Combe and up to the bouldery summit of High Stile. En route the rock changes from the pinky granite, or granophyre, which gives Red Pike its name, to the greyer and more familiar Borrodale volcanic.

High Stile top is rugged, bouldery, and multi-cairned. According to the cartographer a cairn on the north-eastern spur, splitting Bleaberry from Birkness (Burtness) Combe, is one metre higher than the cairned eminence crowning the rim of Chapel Crags, above Bleaberry Combe. West-south-westerly, beyond the head of Ennerdale Water, the Isle of Man may be spotted above the summit of Lank Rigg. From the cairn perched on the very lip of Chapel Crags the 'bird's-eye' view is superb. Below, under the ugly path scar slashing Red Pike, lies dark Bleaberry Tarn. Beyond gleams Crummock Water, split from far

Loweswater by the brawny hump of Mellbreak.

Descend alongside the old fence, south at first, then swinging south-easterly around the rim of Birkness Combe, to ultimately surmount the grassy summit of High Crag. Birkness Combe is not graced by a tarn but lined with magnificent crags which endow it with a special wild beauty. This is climbers' country, from the dank overhangs of Eagle Crag to the sunnier slabs of Grey Crags. Every fellwalker worth his or her salt should make an effort to visit this delectable corrie – one of Lakeland's finest.

By the time you've reached High Crag top, Gable's proud dome – and its pointy underling Green Gable – must be a familiar sight. Marching rightwards of them, above and beyond the bulky plateau of Kirkfell, are Ill Crag, Broad Crag, Scafell Pike and Scafell – three thousand footers all.

Descend south-easterly, still with the occasional fence post, down the steep and badly eroded scree and grass slope of Gamlin End. At the foot of Gamlin End turn left over the rim of the fell and follow a path down alongside walls to join the Scarth Gap path where it passes through a wall gap. Turn left down this, and left at every fork below to join the lakeshore path. Beyond the footbridge over Comb Beck, below where it cascades out of Birkness Combe, the path forks. Take the right fork and every subsequent right fork along this delightful lakeshore path to reach your outward route at the kissing-gate by the water's edge.

The Buttermere Lakeshore Walk

Possibly the finest lakeshore walk in the Lakeland. The path along the Hassness shore is particularly delightful

Parking: As for Walk 1, although it could be as easily done from the Gatescarth car park, see Walk 3.

WALK back between the Bridge Hotel and farm bulidings to the road. Turn right up the road to the entrance to Wilkinsyke Farm, signposted 'Lakeshore Path'. Turn into this, walk past the Sike Farm Shop, and on through the farmyard to a gate labelled 'Footpath'. Beyond this the path crosses fields above the lake. Across the valley Sour Milk Gill spills down the wooded flank of Red Pike. The summit of Red Pike cannot be seen, lying back beyond the rim of Bleaberry Combe. The crenellated crest of High Stile, however, thrusts into view, poised on the rim of Chapel Crags some two thousand three hundred feet above the waters of Buttermere. Red Pike, High Stile and High Crag present to the walker on the Hassness shore a mountain wall almost alpine in stature and structure. A gate is reached signposted 'Bridleway/Lakeshore'. Follow the lakeshore path rightwards to negotiate a steep rocky section before swinging left onto the lake shore. Look back to see the broad summit of Grasmoor rising above conical Whiteless Pike and the lowly but craggy ridge of Rannerdale Knotts.

Across the headwaters of the lake the upland combe of Warnscale Bottom is dominated by the dark tors and crags of Hay Stacks. Beyond a stile a notice informs that you are now on a 'permissive footpath' over private land. This path now wends along the wooded lakeshore, at one point passing through a narrow tunnel hacked through a rocky headland. Up through the trees on your left you will glimpse the cascades of Goat Gill and Hassneshow Beck spilling into impressive ravines. Eventually the path emerges from the trees to cross two flat fields, rounding the wall that divides them by a gate on the lakeshore. Across the lake now Comb Beck spills out of rugged Birkness Combe. In the upper reaches of the combe look for the steep rocks and pointed summit of Eagle Crag. Distance diminishes its size but Eagle Front, a classic 500 foot climb on this crag, was featured in the television series 'Lakeland Rock', being climbed by Chris Bonington and the late Bill Peascod, a pioneer of many superb climbs on the Buttermere crags. Further right, you can now glimpse the summit cone of Red Pike.

A gate leads out of the second field and along a path above the water to shortly emerge on to the road. Turn right, along the road, towards Gatescarth Farm. Ahead rises 'Fleetwith Edge', the steep north-west ridge of Fleetwith Pike. Low down on this ridge you may spot a white cross at the foot of a crag. It marks the spot where an unfortunate Victorian girl lost her life, apparently as a result of tripping over her 'fell-pole'. Fell poles were the Lakeland equivalent of an alpenstock and 'de rigeur' in Victorian fell walking circles, and even earlier. Coleridge felt himself inadequately equipped for a walking expedition without one and virtually wrestled with his wife for her broom handle before setting out. Turn right at Gatescarth Farm through the gate signposted 'Public Bridleway – Ennerdale/Buttermere' and also 'Rescue Post'. Walk between a fence and wall before turning left with the fence to a gate. Beyond this follow a path alongside a wall, then a fence, where there is a contribution box to the Cockermouth Mountain Rescue Team, and into the fields at the head of the lake.

Continue through a gate, over a bridge spanning the Warnscale Beck, then up to and through a gate signposted 'Public Bridleway – Ennerdale via Scarth Gap/Buttermere'. Turn right to follow the latter path to where it crosses a footbridge over Comb Beck, spilling out of Birkness Combe in a series of fine cascades. Beyond the bridge the path forks. Follow the right fork down along the lakeshore to a gate leading into the woods, signposted 'NT Burtness'. Follow a path through woods along the lakeshore to climb to a fork. Turn right and down again to the lakeshore. This path is particularly enjoyable on a clear late winter afternoon or a summer evening, with the Grasmoor fells, gilded with sun and brushed with shadow, rising across the gleaming water. When the path forks right near the end of the lake follow it down to the water's edge to pass through a kissing-gate between a fence and wall. Walk right, across two footbridges spanning becks, and follow the well-worn path right across the fields, to enter Buttermere village past the private car park of the Fish Hotel.

Hay Stacks

Writer after writer has elected this their favourite chunk of mountain Lakeland. The great Wainwright vowed to leave his ashes there. What can I add?

Parking: The car park opposite Gatescarth Farm at the foot of Honister Pass (GR 195150).

CROSS the road to Gatescarth Farm and go through the gate signposted 'Public Bridleway-Ennerdale/Buttermere' and also 'Rescue Post'. Walk between a fence and wall before turning left with the fence to a gate. Beyond this, follow a path alongside a wall, then a fence where there is a contribution box to the Cockermouth Mountain Rescue Team, and into the fields at the head of Buttermere. To your left now your objective looms above Warnscale Bottom. Continue through a gate, over a bridge spanning Warnscale Beck, then up to and through a gate signposted 'Public Bridleway – Ennerdale via Scarth Gap/Buttermere'. Follow the former sign up a steep path alongside a fence to a junction with a crossing path near a fence corner. Turn left up this path. Look left across Warnscale Bottom to spot the old 'slate road' your eventual descent route, slanting across the lower flanks of Fleetwith Pike. Look back down Buttermere to see the broad dome of Grasmoor and conical Whiteless Pike rising above the craggy spur of Rannerdale Knotts. After passing through a gate the path climbs away from its companion old wall and up on to the crest of a ridge between the craggy outcrops of Low and High Wax Knotts. Beyond the ridge the path levels before rising to pass through a gap in a wall. Beyond the gap it climbs leftwards up bouldery ground into an obvious notch in the skyline. Look back to see Grasmoor joined now by pointed Wandope and the domes of Crag Hill and Sail. Above the bouldery climb the path eases leftwards into Scarth Gap, which is crowned by a large cairn to the left of the path just before some old iron fencing. Directly ahead, across the gulf of Ennerdale, thrusts the rugged northeast flank of Kirkfell. Left of Kirkfell rises Great Gable, whilst to the right of it the towering Ennerdale flank of Pillar climbs out of sight behind Seat, a spur of High Crag.

Turn left at the cairn, then shortly left again up an eroded path which serpentines up the rocky fellside. Behind your back, as you

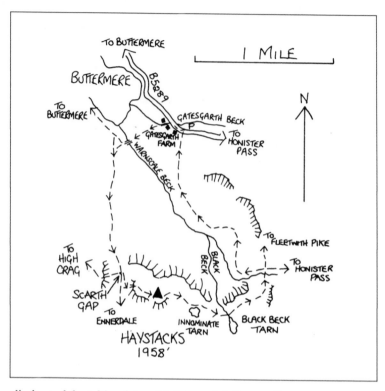

climb, a delectable vista of lakes and fells unrolls away to the far Solway. This gives you every excuse to stop, have a 'breather', turn around and take it all in. Continue on past a 'weeny' tarn and scramble through a belt of rocks to reach an old rusting boundary post, with two more nailing the skyline ahead. Continue in line with these to where some easy scrambling leads up to the second post. Beyond it lies a rocky dip enfolding a tiny tarn. A rocky ridge crowned at each end by a cairn rises beyond. The right hand cairn, the one above the tarn, marks the summit of Hay Stacks. It is in the neighbouring peaks and the lakes spread immediately below that lies the charm of the view from Hay Stacks. South-easterly Gable's dome glowers down the long trough of Ennerdale and its glittering lake. More immediately, across Ennerdale, Kirkfell and Pillar tumble craggy and precipitous flanks into its wooded depths. Search this flank of Pillar for the High Level Route to Pillar Rock. The Buttermere Trio are end-on, so it is the pyramid of High Crag that dominates from here. North-easterly, a distant Skiddaw thrusts between Robinson and Hindscarth, whilst just north of east, Helvellyn rises over the Drum House saddle.

Follow a path behind the cairn into a dip, then climb out of it to follow a path bearing left behind a hummock. This swings right, below rocky hummocks, and down to the shore of Innominate Tarn. Pass to the left of the tarn then follow a path down a steepening hollow. Turn right, under crags and above a drop giving a fine 'bird's eye' view of Warnscale Bottom and the lakes beyond, to cross Black Beck where it exits from Black Beck Tarn. Climb up the shaly far bank, topped by a rocky groove, to easier ground where the path forks. Look back down on to this lovely tarn which is dramatically enhanced by its backcloth of Great Gable and Green Gable.

Take the right fork, following a path behind the rocky hump of Green Crag, with several tiny tarns in a boggy hollow to your right. A boggy dip follows, with a view down into Buttermere in the gap on your left and the pronounced rock mound of Great Round How rising out of the moorland away to your right. Climb up behind another hump, then down, ignoring a path branching right, before swinging left, then right down into a hollow. Cross a beck and climb up to the foot of a crag (Little Round How). Pass below the crag and go down to the bank of Warnscale Beck. The Old Quarry and buildings seen on the opposite fellside are Dubs Quarry. Cross the beck by stepping stones and climb leftwards through the heather along a narrow path traversing across the steep fellside to join a better path. Turn left here. This path once serviced Dubs Quarry. From it there are views down on to the cascades of Warnscale Beck and across to the grim buttresses and gullies of Hay Stacks. Where it swings right, the path becomes more characteristically and delightfully an old quarry road. Built across a steep fellside it becomes positively alpine in character, with the ground falling dramatically away leftwards and crags towering above. Eventually it curves leftwards down on to the floor of the combe where a broad path leads easily back to the Honister Pass road just above the car park.

THREE EASY TWO-THOUSAND FOOTERS

The following three walks are separate ascents of two-thousand footers. All are short up-and-down routes which have the advantage of starting from a car park on the summit of a high road pass. Walks 4 and 5 start from the same place and could easily be combined into one walk if you are feeling energetic. If you are feeling very energetic it would be possible, with a short drive, to combine all three walks into a single expedition, especially on a summer's day. Individually, all are short walks over relatively easy ground giving splendid views, and each is very much worth attempting for its own sake.

Walk 4

Fell Walk
2½ miles/1300 feet of ascent

Dalehead from Honister Pass

Parking: In the National Trust free car park behind the youth hostel on the crest of Honister Pass (GR225135).

CLIMB out of the car park by slate steps and stiles to the left of the youth hostel, following a 'Great Gable/Dubs' sign on to the road. Cross the road to a 'Footpath' sign at the foot of a wood and wire fence climbing the south flank of Dalehead. From the sign climb the path up the left-hand side of the fence to a stile over it. Cross the stile and continue up the right-hand side. Climb easily but steadily alongside the fence, which skirts the rim of an old quarry at one point. The fence ends abruptly about fifteen minutes from the top. The well worn path, liberally piled with cairns, plus the occasional ancient and rusting iron fence post, continues on to where a fine cairn crowns Dalehead's pebbly dome.

When you glimpse the cairn poking over the skyline ahead do not gallop towards it in order to 'bag' it before your companions, especially if the summit is coated with ice or hard snow. You may find yourself freewheeling rapidly past it and into a long slide.

Dalehead's cairn stands on the very lip of the mountain's precipitous north flank. As you step up to it, stretching away below you is one of the finest 'surprise' views in Lakeland. The ground tumbles away into the shadowy depths of Newlands. Your eye travels down the narrow fell corridor, squeezed between Hindscarth and High Spy, to where its

14

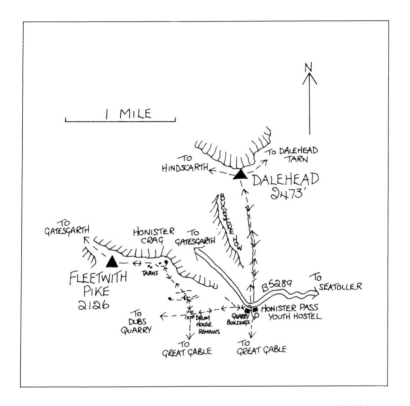

wider, more verdant reaches lead on to Derwentwater and Skiddaw. This magnificent 'surprise' view alone is reward for the modest effort the ascent from Honister entails. The wide-ranging view spread before you as you return down to Honister is a bonus, being equally superb if not quite as dramatically presented. Ranging in a great arc from left to right are High Raise, Harrison Stickle, Pike O'Stickle and Glaramara, the latter a knobbly foreground to Bowfell and a fine Esk Pike. The jumbled massif of Great End and the Scafells leads to the pike of Green Gable, tucked close under Gable's massive dome. Next comes the Beckhead Gap, squat Kirkfell, the gap of Black Sail with Wasdale Red Pike rising beyond it, before the skyline surges skywards in the mass of Pillar. Further right, but closer, the fine Buttermere trio of High Crag, High Stile and Red Pike slant away in echelons of ridge, crag and combe.

Return alongside the fence to your car.

Walk 5   Fell Walk
                                   3½ miles/1000 feet of ascent

Fleetwith Pike from Honister Pass

Parking: As for Walk 4.

CLIMB out of the car park by steps and stiles to the left of the Youth
Hostel, passing a 'Great Gable/Dubs' sign, onto the road. Turn left
and walk down the grass verge to a gate signposted 'Public Bridleway'
leading into the Buttermere Green Slate Quarries. Go through the
gate and walk to the right of the buildings to climb an obvious stony
path slanting rightwards up the fellside. On reaching a junction of
paths signposted 'Advised alternative route Great Gable/Dubs', take
the left-hand path.

To your right towers the industrially ravaged face of Honister Crag.
Until 1914 Honister quarrymen lived, as well as worked, on the
mountain, only visiting their families at weekends. Often they
communicated by carrier pigeon. The Buttermere Green Slate
Company also used this method to pass urgent messages to their Head
Office in Keswick. One wonders what effect the passing peregrine
falcon had on sales of slate!

Across Honister Pass the remnants of an old slate tramway scars
the flank of Dalehead. Prominent to its left is the stark profile of Drum
House Crag on Buckstone How. Beyond and to the left of the crag
looms Hindscarth. Follow your path through a rock cutting and then
in a steady and amazingly straight 'slog' up the fellside. The angle
eases when the path surmounts a large mound that is the remains of
the Drum House, from where trams of slate were once winched down
to the dressing sheds. The early quarrymen used to move up to a
quarter of a ton of slate on sleds, or 'trailbarrows', running before them
like a horse before laboriously hauling the empty sled back uphill.
One Honister quarryman, Joseph Clarke of Stonewaite, is recorded
as having shifted five tons of slate in seventeen journeys.

Viewed from the Drum House, Pillar now rears massively over the
skyline ahead. Below it the summit of Hay Stacks peeks over the rim.
To the right rise High Crag and High Stile. Left of Pillar rises bulky
but unassuming Kirkfell. To your left the Great Gable path climbs
away from the Drum House towards the rocky crest of Grey Knotts.

Leave the Drum House and walk right along a faint path crossing

16

boggy grass to shortly climb on to a quarry road. Turn left up this road, observing an older quarry road alongside and to your right. Shortly, when a building can be seen ahead, look right for two cairns, one on either side of the old road. Turn right now and walk past these cairns to follow a faint cairned path. Look back to see Great Gable's dome now rising above the foothills. Soon your path joins another rough quarry road. Cross this and follow a rough path ahead, passing to the left of a cairn. When a churned-up section swings left you bear right up a path to a cairn. This now frequently-cairned path climbs steadily through heather and rocks. Presently, it levels and a small tarn will be seen filling a hollow ahead, with a glimpse of distant Grasmoor through a gap in the ridge. Now make a short steep climb to your right to reach the cairn crowning Honister Crag (Black Star). The summit of Fleetwith Pike is seen rising a short distance ahead. Beyond and below this lie the beautiful lakes of the Buttermere Valley, with the far Solway gleaming beyond.

Scramble back down to the path and follow it on, passing to the left of the tarn and then around a hummock. More midget tarns are passed on the left before the path twists and undulates up to Fleetwith Pike's fine cairn. Your climb is made worthwhile by the sight of twin lakes spreading below your mountain's north-west ridge.

Immediately below lies Buttermere, split from Crummock Water by the flat alluvial fields around Buttermere village. Buttermere's south-western shore is dominated by the combe-carved flanks of High Crag, High Stile and Red Pike. The opposite shore rises more sedately into the broad rock-scabbed flanks of Robinson and Hindscarth. Between these fells distant Skiddaw and Causey Pike are visible. Crummock Water, from Fleetwith Pike, is dominated by the erosion-slashed flanks of Mellbreak, for brawnier and higher Grasmoor appears to lean back from the lake. Turn your back on this view, and fine fells curve around you from far Helvellyn in the east to the south-westerly and neighbouring mass of Pillar. Lording over this superb crew is Gable's majestic dome, despite higher Scafell trying to get a look in through the Beckhead gap.

Return to your car by your outward route. Shortly after passing Black Star, a faint path may be spotted forking left towards the rim of the crag. From it may be glimpsed airy views down on to galleries hacked out of the crag face. Treat this detour with great caution if conditions are at all slippery.

Robinson From Newlands Hause

Parking: On the grass verges at the crest of Newlands Hause, the high point of the motor road linking Buttermere and the Newlands Valley (GR 193176)

NEARBY Moss Force, spilling down a rocky rim of Robinson, is a popular tourist attraction and worth a visit. Climb the path heading steeply up the right-hand edge of the crags over which Moss Force spills. Eventually a boggy groove leads on to eaiser ground above the crags. Below, to your left, the bleak high valley of Keskadale stretches away towards more verdant Newlands and a distant glimpse of Derwentwater. Ahead of you, the steep summit dome of your objective looms above the broad swampy hollow of Buttermere Moss, the feeding ground of Moss Force. Turn right to climb gently south-westerly up a faint grassy path, following firm ground between the bogs and the rim of the steep fellside falling towards the road where it climbs out of Buttermere. Ahead rises the summit of the spur called High Snockrigg. Shortly your path is joined by the path from Buttermere climbing out of a groove on your right. Around here there is a fine view to you right of Crummock Water, split by the knobbly spur of Rannerdale Knotts, Loweswater and the distant Solway.

Follow this path, which begins to curve left, south-easterly then more easterly, towards the steep final slopes of Robinson. The general objective of the path on this approach to Robinson is to avoid the squelchy hazard of Buttermere Moss. For the most part it succeeds, but the Moss stretches its swampy tentacles wide and before you reach the large cairn at the foot of the Robinson dome you will be very lucky to have escaped!

From this cairn, climb steeply leftwards up a worn slaty groove. The final six hundred feet or so are a bit of a slog, the angle hardly relenting until the summit cairn is reached, perched on a protruding fin of Skiddaw slate. But at least it's dry! Robinson was named after a local Tudor entrepreneur who was quick to grasp the opportunities offered by the dissolution of the monasteries, for the monks held much of Lakeland. The broad summit dome obstructs the valley views but the surrounding display of fells is excellent, particularly Grasmoor and the surrounding peaks across the depths of Newlands Hause.

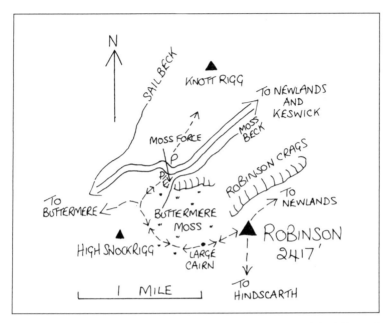

South-westerly the superb triumvirate of Red Pike, High Stile and High Crag tower above dark, glinting Buttermere. A bonus on a clear day is the northern prow of the Isle of Man thrusting around the high shoulder of Red Pike.

Return to your car by the same route.

CRUMMOCK WATER

Walk 7

Medium Walk
3 miles/1000 feet of ascent

Rannerdale Knotts

A short walk, but incorporating interesting terrain, splendid views, and an ancient battleground to boot!

Parking: As for Walk 1.

OPPOSITE the front of the Bridge Hotel, on the left of the bridge over the Mill Beck, is a gate signposted 'National Trust. Ghyll Wood'. Go through this gate and climb the path up the left bank of the charmingly cascaded and wooded beck. Keep left at every fork to eventually reach a gated stile bridging a wall. Cross it onto a path. Walk across this path and follow a path through bracken. At a junction with a crossing path continue ahead up a path eroded into steps. At the next junction, turn right. To your right, across the valley, the road winds up the steep flanks of Robinson on to Newlands Hause. At the next fork climb left up more 'steps'. At the top of the next rise, bear left along a path traversing across the fellside towards the distant knobbly summit of your target. When you round the next corner, Grasmoor and Whiteless Pike loom into view beyond the depths of Rannerdale.

Walk across the crest of the ridge and look down into this lonely mountain defile. Legend has it that the twelfth century fellsmen defenders of Buttermere lured an invading Norman army into Rannerdale to ambush and slaughter. Nicholas Size, formerly mine host at the Bridge Hotel, wrote an entertaining book entitled 'The Secret Valley' which purported to describe the military campaign leading to a bloody finale under Rannerdale Knotts. Novelists Rosemary Sutcliff and Joyce Reason wove their exciting 'The Shield Ring' and 'The Secret Fortress' around the legend. Hard facts to support the legend appear scarce. Cumbria was a 'debatable land', claimed by both Scottish and English kings. It's a grand tale though, appealing to the romantics among us. The derivation of Rannerdale is 'valley of ravens'. Is this another clue about the legendary battle? In medieval ballads, ravens were birds of evil, flesh eaters who thronged

20

to the place of slaughter.

Continue along the ridge, with Crummock Water and Loweswater coming into view to the right of the trio of cairned and rocky tors crowning the ridge. A path skirts leftwards of the rocks but it's much more fun to scramble over them. The furthest appears to be the highest.

South-easterly, Buttermere is ringed by fells, the spike of Honister Crag thrusts above a flank of Robinson, with the more amiable cone of Fleetwith Pike rising to its right. Gable's dominant dome is the eye catcher, however, reducing the 2603 foot Green Gable into relative insignificance. Immediatly below Gable, crenellated Hay Stacks overshadow the combe of Warnscale Bottom. The Beckhead gap, splitting Gable from Kirkfell, is filled by distant Broad Crag, a Scafell Pike satellite. Dumpy Kirkfell is cut off by Buttermere's own High Crag, High Stile and Red Pike.

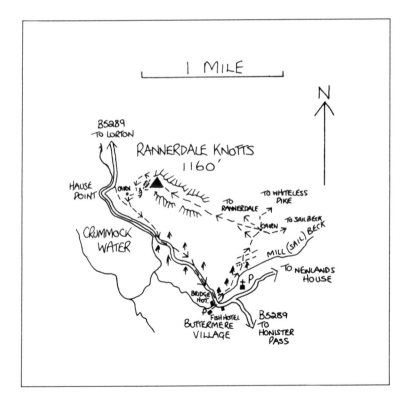

The inimitable Wainwright suggests that conquerers of Rannerdale Knotts should "return by the same route and enjoy the view twice". It's a very brave Lakeland guide book writer who would differ with The Master, and from the aesthetic point of view I wouldn't dream of it. Many fellwalkers, however, love a roundabout route, even if less scenically pleasing, just to widen their knowledge of the fells. For them I offer an alternative descent.

Continue along the ridge to find a 'dyke', or rock cleft or passageway. Go rightwards through this and follow a path which soon twists down leftwards into a rocky hollow (cairn). Now descend right to a lower cairn, then follow a grassy path down through bracken. This bears left on to a steep, stony eroded path slanting leftwards under a crag to reach a cairn on a grass slope. Follow a path slanting left from the cairn through bracken towards a dip in a ridge. Go over the dip and follow a path down through bracken to join a bridleway. Turn left along this and gently across the fellside to reach the lakeshore road shortly before it enters trees. Walk left along the road to where a stony track between fences forks left. Climb up and over this to rejoin the road again and follow it back into Buttermere village.

Whiteside and Hopegill Head

A steepish initial climb is followed by fine ridge walking typical of these lovely north-western fells. With luck, the walker will be able to appreciate splendid views.

Parking: The car park opposite Lanthwaite Green, just south of Lanthwaite Green Farm, on the B5289 (GR 158207).

FROM the car park the impressive mouth of Gasgale Gill can be seen to divide the rugged gully-forked rampart of Grasmoor End from flatish-topped Whiteside. Below Whiteside rises the lower, shapely, and apparently separate peak of Whin-Ben. Your route climbs the Gasgale Gill ridge of Whin-Ben, surmounts its crest and continues on to Whiteside.

Walk leftwards up the road. Just opposite the farm a path marked by a 'Footpath' sign and a broken wood barrier labelled 'No Parking' heads rightwards across Lanthwaite Green. Follow it towards a wall corner. Nearing the corner look for a fainter path forking right. Turn along this to shortly reach a footbridge over the Liza Beck. As you approach the bridge scrutinise the fellside rising beyond it to see an eroded path climbing rightwards from near a wall corner to join a higher grassy path slanting rightwards across the fellside. This path is your target.

Cross the bridge and climb to the higher path. Once upon it, turn right and climb to where, just before it rounds the corner into Gasgale Gill, a steep path forks leftwards near some rocks liberally studded with white quartz. Turn left and climb this path on to the south-west ridge of Whin-Ben. From now on, a worn path climbs through heather mixed with scrub juniper and cowberry on to the crest of Whin-Ben, which proves to be just a lowly spur rather than an isolated peak. A slight dip beyond Whin-Ben leads to the final steepish climb through a belt of markedly striated rocks before the angle eases on to the west summit of Whiteside. From Whin-Ben onwards there are impressive and vertiginous views across a succession of ribs of pallid rock slanting steeply down into Gasgale Gill.

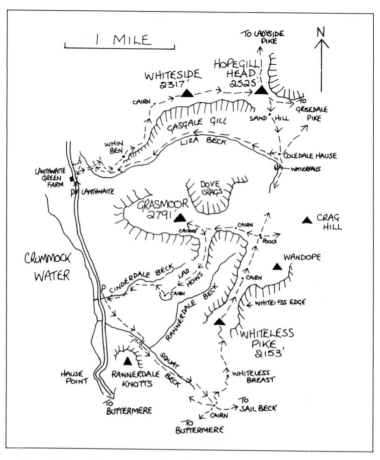

From Whiteside west top there is a wide view of the Solway Plain, Firth, and the hills of lowland Scotland. Away to the west, the Isle of Man should be visible given the right conditions. Across gasgale Gill the massive bulk of Grasmoor blocks the far view. Eastwards, Whiteside undulates away to sharpen up on to Hopegill Head in a blade of ridge that is easier than it looks from here. Walk easily and pleasantly along the ridge towards the cairn-crowned tor of the east summit, the higher by some forty feet. The path tends to run below the crest, along the northern flank. This is a pity, because it actually ignores the sumit and the sensational views down the crumbling aretes and shaly gullies tumbling into Gasgale Gill. To the left, Skiddaw dominates the view ahead. To the right, through the gap of Coledale Hause, Causey Pike thrusts dramatically.

A rocky outcrop guards the start of the graceful summit ridge of Hopegill Head. A path skirts leftwards, but if attacked directly it gives an easy enjoyable scramble. Beware, however, the greasiness of the rock on these fells in wet or damp conditions. Beyond the outcrop, a slender ridge leads delightfully to the summit rocks of Hopegill Head. A proper mountain top this, with its sense of vast space all around. To the north-east rises shapely Grisedale Pike. Southwards, the point of Wandope divides the brawny shapes of Grasmoor and Crag Hill. In the gap to the left of Crag Hill can be seen the distant blue cone of Langdale's Pike O'Stickle.

Close, to the south, stands your next target, the cairn crowning the spur of Sand Hill. Walk down the path bearing south-easterly along the rim of the fell bending towards Grisedale Pike. Shortly, near an obvious notch in the rim to your left, a path forks right. Follow this into a dip, then up to the Sand Hill cairn. From this cairn a path slants just east of south, down scree and grass, to ease on to the broad grassy saddle of Coledale Hause. When the boggy centre of the saddle is reached, walk right to shortly join a path running along the bank of the Liza Beck just below a waterfall. Turn right and follow this path down Gasgale Gill, under the eroded gullies and shattered buttresses of Whiteside, to rejoin your outward route.

Whiteless Pike and Grasmoor

Grasmoor is King of the mountains in the north-west Lakeland. Big, bluff, ruddy, like Henry the Eighth surrounded by a bevy of shapely consorts. There are a variety of interesting ways up and down it. This is not the easiest, nor the hardest, but a good one. You'll enjoy it.

Parking; As for Walk 11, on Cinderdale Common.

START as for Walk 11 as far as the foot of the stile beyond the footbridge over the Rannerdale Beck at the mouth of Rannerdale. Cross the stile and turn left alongside the wall. As you climb up the narrowing valley you realise that this is undoubtly ambush country. If the battle (see Walk 7) did occur, then one has to feel some sympathy for the Norman soldiers, invaders or not, fighting for their lives in wild hostile mountains far from home. Medieval warfare was undoubtly horrifying for men fought eye to eye, hand to hand. I've never felt a sense of horror, or 'bad vibes', walking up Rannerdale, however, even on the gloomiest day. If the horror happened it has been long since exorcised by the 'good vibes' given off by the thousands who have found pleasure and wonderment in exploring Rannerdale and its sublime surrounding fells.

Higher up the valley the path crosses on to the left bank of Squat Beck before surmounting the narrow grassy saddle at its head. A cairn marks the junction of several paths. Ahead, the great bulk of Robinson, rising between the cleft of Newlands Hause and the depths of Buttermere, blocks the view. Look back for a glimpse of Crummock Water, with Loweswater gleaming beyond. Turn left and climb the path zig-zagging steeply upwards. The angle eases when Whiteless Breast is surmounted, but steepens again for the final climb on to the narrow summit of Whiteless Pike.

The views are wide ranging in every direction but northwards, where Grasmoor fills the sky. North-easterly Wandope, Sail, Scar Crags and Causey Pike jut into the valleys of the Sail and Rigg becks. South-south-easterly the distant peaks are of Lakeland's finest. Left to right are Bowfell, Esk Pike, Great End, where the skyline is blocked by Gable's dome, before Scafell Pike and Scafell rear their loftier heads.

The drop into Saddle Gate is followed by the ascent of Whiteless Edge. This 'edge' is a slender ridge with a sense of great depth on either hand but it presents no difficulty that connot be overcome simply by placing one foot in front of the other. It leads to a cairn on a prominence on the south-west corner of the sloping grassy plateau of Wandope Moss, whose summit, Wandope, rises away to your right. Ahead, to your left, looming out of the depths of Rannerdale Beck, and nearly four hundred feet higher, is Grasmoor, your target for today. The fell rising ahead and to your right is Crag Hill.

The path descends slightly before cutting across the slope falling into Rannerdale Beck to reach a junction of paths near some small boggy pools in the grassy saddle between Grasmoor and Crag Hill. Now turn left, west-north-west, and climb a worn path to a large cairn. The path beyond cuts across the head of a shaly slope dropping with increasing steepness towards the Rannerdale Beck. The far side of this slope is bounded by a grassy spur dropping away to your left. This is the head of the Lad Hows ridge, your way down. Pass above the spur and to the right of two prominent cairns to shortly reach the sprawling cairn-cum-wind shelter crowning the summit of Grasmoor, at 2791 feet the highest mountain described in this guidebook.

The view from the summit is so extensive that space does not permit a detailed description. Look down onto the lovely dark gleaming lakes set in a ring of fells that time and weather have carved and polished into a rare finish, and visualise the twelfth century 'secret fortress'. Curiously, from here, Gable's usually dominant dome merges into the rugged backcloth of the loftier Scafells. If the day is fine, walk north-easterly across the summit plateau to reach the rim of Dove Crags. Across the gulf of Gasgale Gill the deeply eroded gullies of Whiteside, spewing ashen scree, would make a fitting backcloth to a 'spaghetti' western.

To descend, retrace your steps until you have passed to the left of the second sizeable cairn perched on the fell rim. Now turn right on to the grassy spur which steepens into a stony ridge. Despite the rough ground underfoot there is a reasonable twisty path. This steep stony ridge eventually eases out into a broader heathery spur where the path becomes less obvious. Continue to where the butt-end of the spur is crowned by a small cairn. From it, bear down to the right on an improving path twisting down through the bracken to ultimately follow the tinkling cascades of Cinderdale Beck down to Cinderdale Common and your car.

It is no doubt obvious to readers of this book that Walks 8 and 9 could be easily linked together to make a longer and undoubtedly rewarding walk.

Scale Force

An easy half-day walk to see Lakeland's highest single waterfall. Especially good views en route of the fells overlooking Crummock Water. A walk giving ample time and opportunity for flower spotting and bird and mountain watching.

Parking: As for Walk 1.

FOLLOW the path to the left of the Fish Hotel private car park. Through the trees on the lower slopes of Red Pike, across the fields ahead of you, can be glimpsed the cascades of Sour Milk Gill – not Scale Force.

At the first fork, turn right through a gate signposted 'Scale Bridge/ Scale Force'. Hump-backed Scale Bridge spans Buttermere Dubs, the beck linking the valley's lakes. Cross it and turn right at a 'Buttermere Lake/Scale Force' sign, alng a stony, sometimes boggy, path through sparse woodland to eventually cross a footbridge over Far Ruddy Beck. The path begins to steepen a little as it climbs leftwards across more open ground. To your right, across Crummock Water, the skyline is dominated by Grasmoor and Whiteless Pike. Both spill steep shaly flanks into the secret valley of Rannerdale (see Walk 7), hidden by the spine of Rannerdale Knotts. Where the ground becomes boggier, a line of cairns leads directly up hill to the left, before contouring right to eventually reach the footbridge spanning Scale Beck below the mouth of the gloomy cleft enfolding Scale Force.

If the flow of water allows it, for the best view of the fall enter the ravine and scramble up a prominent rib of pinky rock close under its left wall to reach the pool at the foot of the cascade. A sketch in Wainwright's 'Western Fells' shows a ladder propped against this rib, obviously to help the less athletic get to close quarters with Scale Force. I'm sorry to say that the ladder must have been demolished years ago by the constant clamber of countless pairs of boots. The rock is solid, however, and the holds 'juggy' – 'large' in climbing parlance.

I've been unfortunate in that I have only seen Scale Force on dull, overcast days, but as Lakeland's highest cascade (125 feet or so) it is

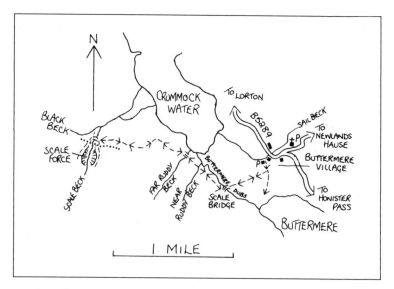

worth a first time visit whatever the conditions. The walk is not particularly strenuous, if a little squelchy, and gives fine views of Crummock Water and the surrounding fells.

Return to you car by your outward route. (This walk can be used as a variation start to Walk 1. After visiting the fall climb the steep path up either bank to eventually emerge onto Lingcomb Edge and ultimately onto Red Pike.)

A Crummock Walkabout

*Don't be deterred by my frequent reference to bogs in this description.
A price to pay for exploring Lakeland's lovely fells and valleys is damp
feet, but the effort is worth every squelchy toe in every soggy sock.
So is this interesting walk of ever-changing views.*

*Parking: In either of the two car parks on Cinderdale Common,
below Grasmoor (GR163194). If you park in the car park signposted
'Cinderdale Car Park' near a litter bin and a 'Footpath' fingerpost,
follow the footpath heading out of the back of the car park and across
the common to where an obvious path fords Cinderdale Beck. If you
are in the smaller car park at the foot of Cinderdale Beck, walk up
alongside the beck to the same point.*

CROSS the beck and climb the path slightly leftwards towards a
rounded tree-topped crag on the skyline. Pass below this and continue
towards the narrow valley of Rannerdale, its mouth dominated by
the craggy pyramid of Rannerdale Knotts. As you enter the mouth
of Rannerdale the path forks near an upright metal sign 'Path'. Turn
right here and cross a footbridge over Rannerdale Beck. Then climb
up to the foot of a stile over a wall. Do not cross the stile but turn right
to follow a path alongside the beck. This path shortly swings away
from the beck to reach a kissing-gate in a wall corner. Go through
this and follow a path alongside a wall under the steep craggy face
of Rannerdale Knotts, to reach the road. Turn left along the road to
see two 'green' paths slanting up the fellside to your left from a
'Footpath/Bridleway' sign. Climb the left-hand 'footpath'. As you
climb observe two rocky humps on the skyline above, the right-hand
one crowned by a tree. The gap between them is your target. Follow
the broad green path until it becomes boggy, then climb left up grassy
'steps' on to a firmer path slanting right towards the gap. Climb left
through the gap, passing across a worn rock slab, then continue ahead
across a narrow beck before climbing right over another 'hollowed'
slab. These polished rocks could be the effect of ancient traffic, for
this was the old road over Hause Point before the construction of the
present motor road. Beyond the second slab, the path forks. Take the
left fork on to a crest.

Now the mountains encircling Buttermere array themselves before you. Leftwards from conical Red Pike, directly opposite across the head of Crummock Water, are High Stile and High Crag. Then Gable's dome dwarfing the tiny pike of Green Gable, both towering over the lowlier Hay Stacks. Further left, rise the double cones of Fleetwith Pike and Honister Crag.

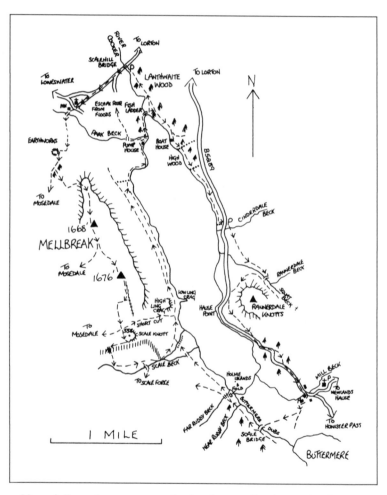

Now follow the grassy path slanting easily down the brackeny fellside to reach the road. Follow the road leftwards through woods. At a right-hand bend, fork left up and over a stony fenced lane to rejoin the road. Turn left and follow it down into Buttermere village, ignoring a 'Crummock Lake/Buttermere Village' sign on your right. Take the fenced path to the left of the Fish Hotel. The waterfall spilling down the tree covered flank of Red Pike ahead is Sour Milk Gill. At the first fork, turn right through a gate signposted 'Scale Bridge/Scale Force'. Follow this path across the fields to cross Scale Bridge where it spans Buttermere Dubs, the beck linking the lakes. Beyond Scale Bridge turn right at a sign 'Buttermere Lake/Scale Force'. This stony path crosses Near Ruddy Beck, which empties into Buttermere Dubs, and Far Ruddy Beck, spanned by a footbridge, which empties into Crummock Water opposite the small wooded Holme Islands. Just before reaching Far Ruddy Beck look for a footpath forking right to cross this beck below the footbridge and to the left of a sheepfold. Follow this fork over the beck to twist across boggy ground through stands of predominantly holly trees. A particularly squelchy patch is reached which you may have to avoid by climbing up the fellside. Also around here a path climbs leftwards towards Scale Force. Do not follow this path, always aim for the distant hump-ended promontory of Low Ling Crag and its guardian High Ling Crag. Beyond the 'squelch' a footbridge spans a tributary of Scale Beck, followed by a path across firmer brackeny ground leading to a gap in a wall on the bank of Scale Beck.

Cross by stepping stones. There is a footbridge, but it is a considerable way upstream. Beyond Scale Beck, follow the lakeshore path to pass between High Ling Crag and the Promontory of Low Ling Crag – an idyllic spot for a picnic and swim. Across the lake towers massive Grasmoor, its Lads How ridge curving down between the ravines of Cinderdale and Rannerdale Becks. Whiteless Pike can be seen above the craggy crest of Rannerdale Knotts, both peaks enfolding the once bloody defile of Rannerdale (see Walk 7).

Beyond the promontory, the path passed below the precipitous Crummock flank of Mellbreak and subsequently through the drainage from the broad summit domes above. It's a bit squelchy hereabouts. There are two parallel paths - the higher is the drier! As you go you will see that the upper path climbs leftwards towards the top of a wall climbing the fellside ahead. Your target, however, is an obvious gap in the foot of that wall close to the lake shore. Keep with the upper path to where the path forks right down to the gap, which is blocked by a stile. Cross this stile and follow a path around the shore to a stile over a wall. Beyond this, walk around a lovely little bay giving a superb view up the length of Crummock Water to Hay Stacks and Gable. Beyond the bay, climb over a sparsely wooded promontory then leftwards down the grassy lake bank to a stile. Beyond this the path keeps to the left and below a concrete flood barrier. Recently we were forced to slosh along the top of this barrier which was awash with flood water. Our crossing wasn't helped by a sly gusty wind. This barrier/path leads to a fenced-off pump house. Move left around the fence to cross a stile. Beyond this follow the wooded and concrete-lined lakeshore. Cross a footbridge over the Park Beck, which channels overspill from Loweswater into Crummock Water, before continuing along the lakeshore to reach the Fish Ladder.

The spillway is crossed by two footbridges linked by an island. On the same December evening we were forced to paddle along the rim of the flood barrier, we found this island under roaring waist high water. We had to beat a retreat to the pump house and detour around the Scalehill road bridge before heading back through Lanthwaite Wood in gathering darkness to finally reach the far side of the Fish Ladder, an extra mile and a half on.

All being well, you cross the Fish Ladder, walk to the right of two lakeside seats, and climb a path up into the trees to join a crossing path. Turn right and follow this to a fork. Go down to the right behind a boathouse then bear left to a stone stile leading into High Wood. Recently, felling has been in progress here, but by the time you read this all the debris should have been cleared away. Follow a path close to the lakeshore to another stone wall stile in the far boundary of High Wood. Continue along a lakeshore path through less thickly wooded ground, passing over frequent footbridges and stiles, until an unbreached wall looms ahead. Turn left and climb a stepped path alongside the wall to reach a stile leading onto the road signposted 'Public Footpath/Scale Hill' on its farther side. Turn right down the road shortly to reach your car.

Mellbreak

When approached from Scalehill Bridge, Mellbreak appears as a towering, weather-ravaged cone that belies its modest height. Get closer and it soars even steeper. Lock grips with it and you'll find the climb up its northern prow steep but full of interest. The summit is a disappointment, but the climb and unfolding views are worth every gasping breath.

Parking: In the National Trust free car park in Lanthwaite Wood, near Scalehill Bridge, on the road between Lorton and Loweswater. (GR 149215)

WALK back on to the road and turn over the bridge. Ignore the first fork left and continue to where the road forks by a telephone box. Mellbreak towers ahead, an exciting challenge. Peer over the hedges to your left for a glimpse of Gable's far dome crowning the head of the valley. Over your left shoulder loom Whiteside and Grasmoor. Turn left at the telephone box and walk down past the church to a junction. Turn down left and almost immediately right, following a 'No Through Road' sign, to pass behind the Kirkstile Inn. Shortly, cross a bridge over Park Beck. The tarmac ends by Kirkgate Farm. Continue up the rough walled lane. When you've turned right up a long straight 'kink' in the lane, pause and look back across the valley to the towering face of Grasmoor End, slashed by the distinctive Y-shaped Lorton Gully. Gasgale Gill rises in its shadow to culminate in the shapely form of Hopegill Head. Bulky Whiteside forms the northern rampart of this mountain defile. Where the lane turns back into line look into the field to your right to see some ill-defined grassy humps. These are ancient earthworks which appear more purposeful when seen from above. Try and remember to pick them out when high on the fell. The lane ends at a gate, beyond which paths fork.

Climb steeply left between trees to emerge on to the open fellside and a crossing path. Cross this and follow a path climbing directly up through bracken towards the foot of the looming mass of rock, scree and heather above. It ends near a cairn at the foot of a fan of pinky scree. Pause here for a breather. Look back on to Loweswater nestling in its woody hollow. Beyond, the hills of lowland Scotland are visible over the Solway. Now climb a path slanting up the scree to your left to reach a heather slope. Turn right, following a path climbing alongside the heather. When you join a scree fan, turn left and climb through the heather alongside it. Just above where the scree squeezes between heathery banks a path slants left. It zig-zags across and around patches of scree before slanting leftwards towards an obvious pinnacle on the skyline. Turn the pinnacle on to its left and climb the crest of a rocky ridge on to level ground near a cairn. Turn left and climb through steep heather on to the crest of a ridge. Here a path forks left onto a ledge giving a 'surprise view' of Crummock Water and Buttermere that makes all your efforts worthwhile. The 'hard bit' is over now. Step back on to the ridge path and follow it up easy-angled slopes shortly to reach the two cairns crowning the disappointingly broad and grassy northern summit of Mellbreak.

Northwards, there is a panoramic view of the Solway, South-easterly, over and beyond the fell's southern top, is High Stile, with Red Pike's cone to its right. Behind Red Pike peeks Pillar. To the left of High Stile looms Gable, the V-gash of Windy Gap, and Green Gable. Below and left of Gable, Hay Stacks and Fleetwith Pike curve around the headwaters of Buttermere. Across Crummock Water, the medieval battleground of Rannerdale (see Walk 7) lies in the shadow of the rocky spur of Rannerdale Knotts. Walk a little way east of the cairns for the view down to Crummock Water, dominated by the massive pinky-grey dome of Grasmoor.

Mellbreak's south top, an equally broad and grassy dome some eight feet higher, lies across a wide boggy saddle. To capture it, follow a cairned path down into the saddle. When this path begins to veer right, down towards Mossdale, turn left up a fainter path. (Should you wish to cut short your walk, continue down the right-hand path into Mossdale, where a right turn will take you back to the gate at the head of the walled lane.) The left-hand path is indistinct and should you lose it simply head uphill to find the cairn. As you climb look right, between Great Borne and Hen Comb, to see, if you're lucky, the Isle of Man.

Descend alongside a decrepit old fence. When this drops steeply left follow a faint path curving right, then dropping steeply left. Look below to see this path continuing through a belt of bracken. Head down to it to emerge beyond the bracken onto a crossing path behind a rise marked as 338 metres or Scale Knott on the 2½" map. The quickest route from this point down to the lakeshore path is to turn left and descend steep slopes of bracken and grass. If you do not fancy such a knee-jellying descent and prefer something less arduous, if longer, then read on.

Go to the right of the rise and descend a faint path leftwards above a boggy hollow. Continue over a slight rise then down to a fence. Turn right and follow the fence to reach two stiles. Cross the first and follow a fence down to join a path near a stile. Turn left down this increasingly boggy path along the left bank of Black Beck to reach a stile near a fence corner and a gate. Cross the stile and turn left past the fence corner, following Scale Beck to where the lakeshore path crosses it. Turn left along this path to shortly pass between High Ling Crag and the promontory of Low Ling Crag – an idyllic spot for a picnic and swim. (Now follow the description in Walk 11 from "Across the lake towers massive Grasmoor" to "an extra mile and a half on".)

Across the Fish Ladder bridges, go past a wooden seat and turn left up a path through the trees to a fork. Turn left again and walk through Lanthwaite Wood to eventually reach you car. Should flood conditions prevent you crossing the Fish Ladder return to and cross the bridge over Park Beck. Now turn right and walk alongside Park Beck to another footbridge. Cross back over the beck and follow a path through the fields to Muncaster House and on up the farm road to a junction with your outward route just beyond Scalehill Bridge.

WHINLATTER PASS

Walk 13

Fell Walk
7 miles/2100 feet of ascent

Hopegill Head and Grisedale Pike

A somewhat tortuous start through forest, but once the crest is gained yet another delightful ridge walk unfolds ahead. At first glance, the summit ridge of Hopegill Head may give pause for thought, but what you don't fancy you can easily avoid. Think twice, however, if the mountain is sheathed in hard snow or ice and you have neither the gear nor the experience needed.

Parking: In the Visitor Centre Car Park on the crest of Whinlatter Pass (GR 207245).

WALK back on to the road and turn right. Walk just under a mile down the road to a forest road entrance on your left. Turn into the entrance and almost immediately right at a junction of forest roads. Climb over a rise then go down to a concrete bridge over the Hobcarton Gill, passing the entrances to forest roads 35 and 36. Rising above the trees on your left now is Ladyside Pike, crowned by its massive cairn. Cross the bridge and climb a forest road, zig-zagging up right then left to a junction. Ignore the road numbered 37 climbing right and continue leftwards, or straight ahead as it may seem to you, to eventually reach a gate at the edge of the forest.

Go through the gate and a ramshackle sheep pen and follow a faint path slanting across the fellside towards and past and old sheepfold. Just beyond the sheepfold look to your right to see a path slanting right up the steep fellside. Climb this, passing through the weathered husks of ancient trees, to reach a fence corner. Climb over the fence to your left, then directly up the grassy fellside ahead, ignoring faint paths bearing left and right alongside the fence. Continue climbing, passing an occasional rusting iron fencepost, until the angle eases and the slope descends to abut an old wall and a wood and wire fence. The Whiteside-Hopegill Head ridge now looms into view beyond Ladyside Pike. Turn left and follow a path alongside the wall/fence to reach a

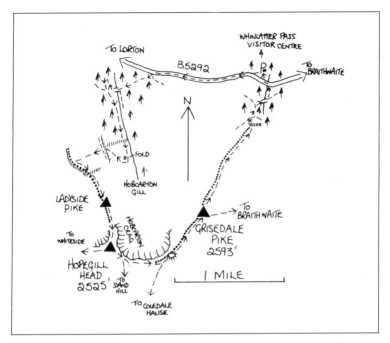

stile in a crossing fence. Cross this and climb up the steepish grass ridge that brings you to the handsome cairn crowning Ladyside Pike.

The ridge ahead dips then rises steeply in challenging, some may think threatening, rocky ramparts to the summit of Hopegill Head. Do not worry, its bark is worse than its bite. Descend easily into the dip then up to the first slaty rock tower. All apparent difficulties can be avoided by simply moving to the right to eventually enter a shallow grove or fault line which leads easily up to the summit. If the rock is dry, however, it's fun to scramble up the rocks and keep left and as close as you can bear to the airy rim of Hobcarton Crag. This will lead you onto a slabby platform and across a substantial notch to a delightful finish up a narrow rocky ridge. Hopegill Head is a true mountain top, being the ultimate junction of fine ridges. (For particulars of the view from here see Walk 8.)

Descend left, south-easterly, at first, then gradually swinging east, along the path following the rim of the fell, or sometimes just below it, into a dip. From a rocky pulpit on the rim of the dip, look back with some amazement at the spectacular profile of the ridge you have just climbed and its equally spectacular position poised over Hobcarton Crag. Despite its dizzying splendour Hobcarton Crag fails to attract climbers because its rock is too friable. Only a kamikaze botanist could be lured on to its vertiginous 'grot' in search of the rare Red Alpine Catchfly, or Viscaria Alpina, which has been reported clinging to its crumbly ledges.

Climb out of the dip alongside an old wall. Follow it up to and over a rocky hump bestriding the ridge. Descend shortly beyond before climbing alongside the wall up the shaly and steepening ridge that leads on to the narrow summit of Grisedale Pike. It's been my experience to find this summit one of the windiest in Lakeland. I'm not alone in this. One winter day a friend of mine was crossing it when he was hit by a blast so fierce it ripped his specs away, hurling them into the depths.

The view is extensive in every direction, virtually everything that is anything can be spotted. Notable exceptions are High Street, Coniston Old Man and Pillar, which are hidden by obtruding fells. The summit is a good spot for spending time with your map orientating yourself with Lakeland's sykline. Pick a calm day though or your map may join David's specs somewhere in the depths of Coledale.

To descend, continue past the summit cairn alongside the old wall towards a rusting fence stanchion. To the right of this, a cairn marks the start of the way down to Braithwaite. The wall turns left, north, at the stanchion, before shortly veering on to the mountain's north-east ridge. Follow an easy path alongside the wall down this grassy ridge to a fence at the edge of the forest. Cross the fence by a stile and move left on to a forest road. Turn right and follow this down to a fork. Turn left, uphill, at the fork. At the next fork, turn right and down to cross a bridge over the Sanderson Gill. Climb up the far slope then fork left towards the Whinlatter Pass road. Fork left again to reach the road. Turn left up the road and across Comb Bridge. Just beyond the bridge a path climbs right through the trees providing a short cut to the Visitor Centre Car Park.

Barf and Lord's Seat

*An ascent of Barf by the 'direct' route is not for the faint-hearted.
Still, it's great fun. Should such steep rough ground be a first for you,
you can proudly utter, as you totter to the cairn – "Great things are
done when men and mountains meet".*

*Parking: Follow the A66 from Keswick towards Cockermouth as far
as the turn off for Thornthwaite. Follow this minor road through
Thornthwaite to reach the National Trust free car park at Powter
How, on the right just past the Swan Hotel (GR 221265).*

WALK back to the road and cross it on to a tarmac strip signposted
'Lord's Seat/Barf'.

Direct Route

Shortly you will see a gate in the fence to your right. Go through this
and follow a path leftwards to reach the whitewashed stone called The
Clerk. Immediately above, crowning a steep scree slope, stands the
whitened monolith known as The Bishop. Climb directly up towards
it. It's a steep pull, and whoever tackles this slope whilst lugging a
bucket of whitewash to clothe His Grace in fresh vestments has my
utmost admiration. The scree is not of the ankle-twisting variety,
being of fine texture which does tend to consolidate after you've slid
backwards a foot or so. To lose hard earned height, however, after
every upward stagger is somewhat frustrating. When flopped at The
Bishop's feet, and the red mist clears, you will notice Skiddaw rising
grandly to your left, whilst below your toe caps marshy flats stretch
away towards the rooftops of Keswick and a backcloth of the domes
of the Helvellyn Dodds.

Climb behind The Bishop up a steepish gully of slithery shale and
suspect rock. Near the top, move left on to easier heathery ground,
then right towards a solitary rowan tree carved with lovers' entwined
initials. Follow a path behind the rowan slightly down into a scree-
filled hollow. Turn right along a path following the foot of the scree
which shortly climbs left to the foot of another scree patch. Climb
directly across this to join a path climbing through the heather above
towards the greenish rocks of Slape Crag. This path slants left to
emerge at the foot of the scree below Slape Crag. Walk left along the

foot of the scree, then rightish across a shaly slope, to rocks below and to the left of Slape Crag where an oak and rowan grow.

Now traverse leftwards, above the trees, and around a corner. Beyond this the path contours across the fellside towards where an obvious pinnacle marks the edge of the crags above. Ignore a path

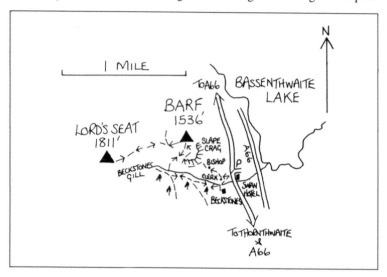

forking right a short way beyond the traverse. Climb up towards the edge of the crag, passing close to the pinnacle, then walk right along a path following the rim of the crag. At the highest point of the crag climb leftwards through the heather on to the crest above. Climb towards a further crest to join a good path climbing up from your left (the ordinary route). Turn right and follow this on to the crest to be greeted by a magnificent 'bird's eye' view of Bassenthwaite Lake. The next crest is the summit of Barf, crowned by a small cairn to the right of the path. From here, the massive ramparts of Skiddaw rise relentlessly above Bassenthwaite Lake. The wooded cone of Dodd is backed by the scree-streaked dimples of Longside Edge and Carlside, with the high dome of Skiddaw and its lower but shapelier Low Man rising beyond.

Ordinary Route

Continue up the tarmac strip past the gate leading to the direct route. Where the tarmac curves left towards the entrance to the buildings of Beckstones walk right to a stile in a fence corner. Cross this and follow a path bearing right to the foot of a shaly slope. Bear right along a path climbing through trees. When a path forks left towards the end of a forest road ignore it. Higher, your path makes an interesting traverse to the right across the face of a small vegetated crag. Climb on through the woodland above to emerge onto a forest road near a cairn. Turn right along this road which shortly steepens leftwards. Look for a path turning right towards a stile at the forest edge. Cross the stile, then Beckstones Gill, and follow a good path slanting right across the heathery fellside to join the direct route just below Barf summit.

Lord's Seat

From Barf head west along a path skirting around humps and dipping into boggy hollows before reaching a fork. Take the left fork which slants leftwards across the fellside to emerge on to the north-east ridge of Lord's Seat near a swamp at the foot of the grassy summit cone. From Lord's Seat top there's a splendid view of the Solway with dominant Criffel rising beyond. Closer, south-south-westerly, rise the shapely duo of Grisedale Pike and Hopegill Head.

Return by the same route to Barf and then reverse the 'ordinary' route back to your car.

A Coledale Horseshoe

The hardest fell walk in this book, but given good conditions, not excessively arduous. A walk over some of the most graceful fells in Lakeland giving magnificent views. Good paths all the way to ease your navigation. You can 'escape' easily from two points if the weather breaks (or you do!) Pick a nice day and give it a go – it's a 'cracker'!

Parking: In a small car park, on the left, just above where the Whinlatter Pass road begins to climb steeply out of Braithwaite, and where it's joined by the rough Coledale mines road (GR 227237). If it is full, there is space further up the road.

TAKE the path climbing to the right out of the rear of the car park, eventually to slant up to the left to reach the crest of the grassy shoulder called Kinn. Kinn is German for 'chin' and a relic perhaps of the Augsburg miners imported into the area by Hochstetter in Elizabethan times. These skilled, travelled and highly paid foreigners were an attraction to local girls, causing some disenchantment amongst Tudor Cumbrian males. There were ugly scenes and at least one murder, and for a time the Germans were lodged on Derwent Isle for their own safety. Eventually they became accepted and inter-married. Beck, Moser, Calvert, Raisley and Caryus are just a handful of the anglicised German names surviving in Cumbria.

The route is obvious now. The cairn crowning Grisedale Pike is just under two miles walk and a fifteen hundred foot climb away and is reached by a final steep pull up a shaly ridge. As you go, there are fine views to the south across the gulf of Coledale. The northern aspect is marred by regimented conifers, their dark uniformity blotched by scabrous clearings. The summit view widens to embrace the Solway Firth and lowland Scotland. Across the Hobcarton valley is the challenging profile of Hopegill Head.

Head south-westerly down a stony ridge alongside an old wall. Climb over a rocky hump and follow the wall into a dip. Beyond the right-hand rim of the dip the crumbly buttresses of Hobcarton Crag are crowned by the spectacular summit ridge of Hopegill Head. (See Walk 13 re Hobcarton Crag.) Turn left out of the dip and follow a path down on to the grassy saddle of Coledale Hause, passing en route

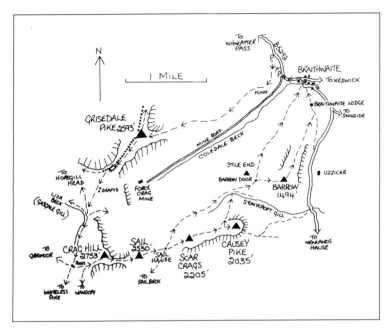

some old fenced-off mine shafts. If desired you could 'escape' at Coledale Hause by turning left and following a path down to the old Force Crag Mine buildings and then along the old mine road back to your car.

To continue, climb southerly up a path passing above and to the left of a waterfall, into the grassy hollow between Crag Hill and Grasmoor. Climb alongside the headwaters of the Liza Beck and on until the angle eases and a junction of paths is joined near some small boggy pools. Turn left, east, here and climb a path up steepening grass which shortly eases onto the summit dome of Crag Hill. As you reach the trig-point the ground ahead falls steeply away to reveal a splendid panorama of the Vale of Derwentwater. Gable, backed by the three-thousand footers of the Scafell range, peers over the far south-south-easterly rim of your summit. Further right Pillar, Scoatfell and Haycock peek over the Buttermere trio of High Crag, High Stile and Red Pike.

Walk to the right, along the rim of the fell to its south-east corner, to reach a cairn marking the descent on to The Scar, a slender and nicely rocky ridge linking Crag Hill and Sail. This is the narrowest section of the walk and there are a couple of rock steps to clamber down, but unless it is plastered in ice and snow and there is a Force

Ten gale blowing you shouldn't have any difficulty. The summit of Sail is a heathery dome crowned by a small cairn a few yards to the left of the path. Walk past the cairn to the fell edge for an impressive view of the craggy north-east flank of Crag Hill. Directly across the great bowl of Coledale the south-east flank of Grisedale Pike falls seventeen hundred feet in a sweep of relenting steepness from narrow summit to the decrepit buildings of Force Crag Mine. Barytes was mined here and the mine has been spasmodically operational in fairly recent times. From Sail summit a badly eroded path leads down to the boggy saddle of Sail Hause.

Sail Hause is your second 'escape' route, should you wish to do so. Turn left down a narrow path slanting across the shaly flank of Scar Crags above the upland hollow of Long Comb, where cobalt was once mined, cross the grassy plateau of High Moss, passing a sheepfold, and continue down the former miners track on the left bank of Stonycroft Gill. The three fells rising on your left are Outerside, Stile End and Barrow respectively. Your target is Barrow Door, the gap between Stile End and Barrow. When roughly below a sheepfold on your left, look for a path left up the fellside towards Barrow Door. Climb this up to and through Barrow Door and follow the path down the far side, alongside Barrow Gill, back to Braithwaite and ultimately your car.

If, at Sail Hause, you are still feeling energetic, continue along the ridge by climbing up on to the broad boggyish ridge of Scar Crags. Beyond the summit of Scar Crags a shallow dip is followed by the bumpety ridge whose last rocky burp is the summit of Causey Pike.

To descend, walk back along the ridge into the dip below Scar Crags, then turn right down the grassy slope into Stonycroft Gill. There is no path but it is perfectly safe, although by the time you have forded the gill and climbed on to the old miners track on the far bank your knees might feel a bit wobbly. Now look for the path slanting left up into Barrow Door, as in the already described 'escape' route.

Should you still be feeling fairly frisky, don't go straight down to Braithwaite from Barrow Door, turn right and make the short climb to the summit of Barrow. It's worth the effort just to look back with justifiable pride at the splendid fell skyline you have traversed. Turn the other way and the lush pastoral beauty of Newlands spreads away towards gleaming Derwentwater. The medieval Cistercian monks created their 'neulandes' by draining Husaker Tarn, the name and site lingering still in Uzzicar Farm, almost immediately below your toecaps.

Turn left and descend the heathery ridge to reach a crossing path close to the edge of a wood, which leads left to Braithwaite Lodge Farm. Follow the farm road down into Braithwaite for the final taxing but short climb back to your car.

Should weather or ground conditions deter you from the pathless descent from Causey Pike into Stonycroft Gill, continue along the ridge. Descend the steep rocks beyond the summit then down easier ground to a path fork. Descend the left fork, slanting down the fellside to emerge on to the tarmac road near Stonycroft Bridge. Turn left across the bridge and along the road, eventually passing the fence below the steep eroded flank of Barrow, to a path on your left, signposted 'Public Bridleway – Braithwaite'. Climb this path to eventually join the previously described descent from Barrow close to Braithwaite Lodge Farm.